W9-AGX-035

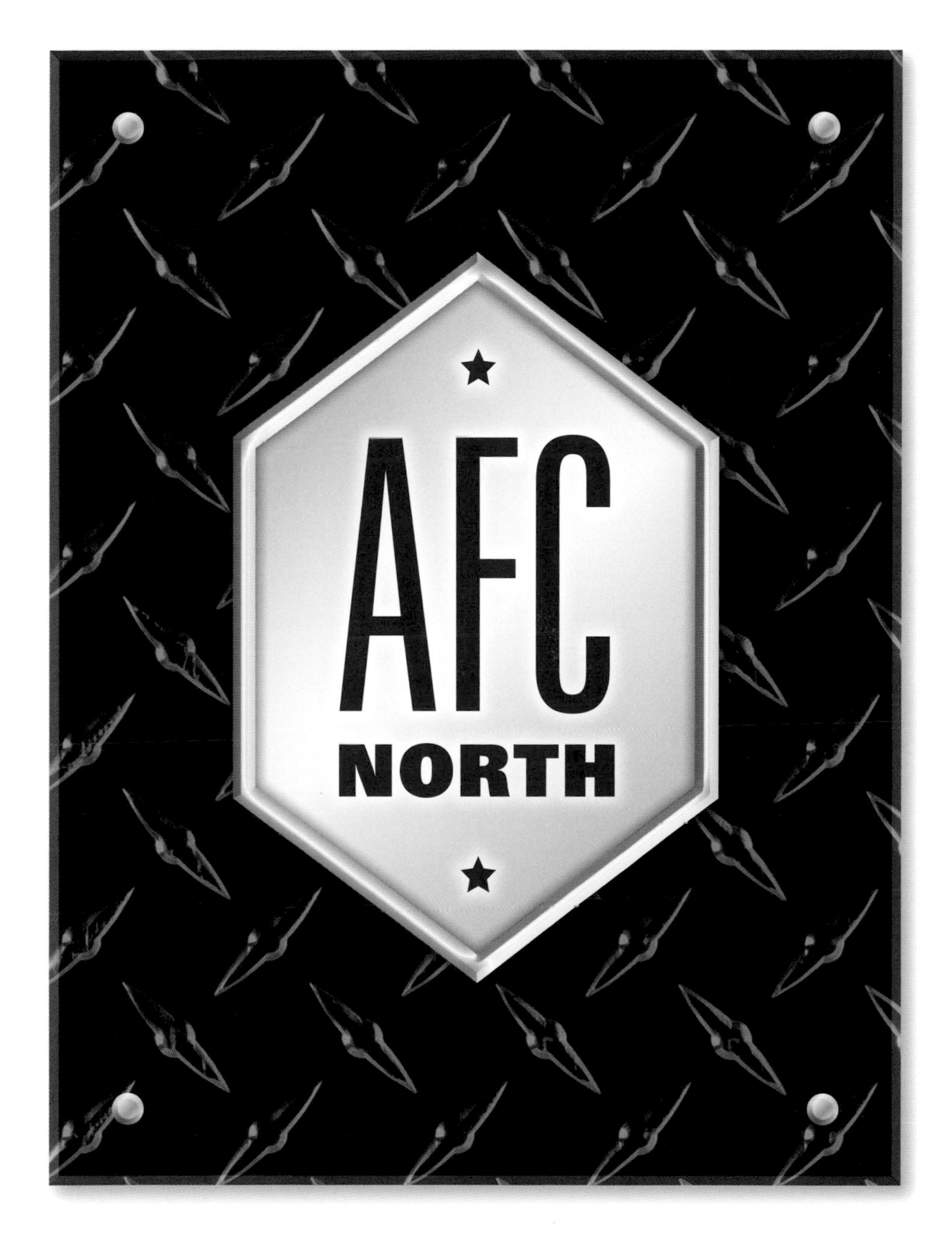

BY JIM GIGLIOTTI

★ Baltimore Ravens ★ Cincinnati Bengals ★ Cleveland Browns ★ Pittsburgh Steelers ★

Published by The Child's World®
1980 Lookout Drive
Mankato, MN 56003-1705
800-599-READ
www.childsworld.com

The Child's World®: Mary Berendes, Publishing Director
The Design Lab: Kathleen Petelinsek, Design
Editorial Directions, Inc.: Pam Mamsch and E. Russell Primm, Project Managers

Photographs ©: Robbins Photography (except page 13, AP)

Library of Congress Cataloging-in-Publication Data
Gigliotti, Jim.
AFC North / by Jim Gigliotti.
p. cm. Includes bibliographical references and index.
ISBN 978-1-60973-128-1 (library reinforced : alk. paper)
1. American Football Conference—Juvenile literature.
2. Football—Northeastern States—Juvenile literature. I. Title.
GV950.7.G537 2011
796.332'640973—dc22 2011007401

Printed in the United States of America
Mankato, MN
May, 2011
PA02093

★

TABLE OF CONTENTS

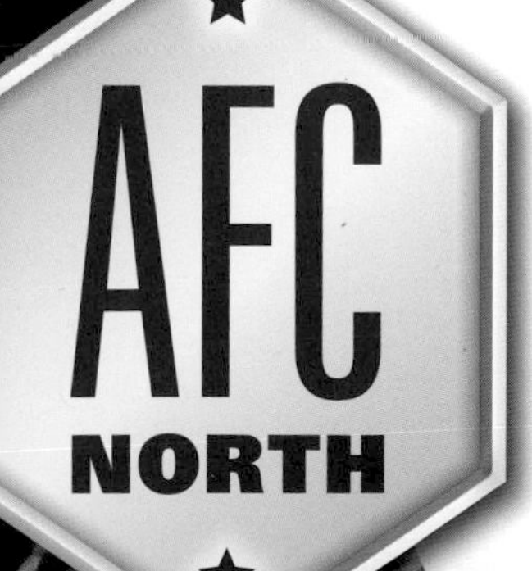

First Season: 1996
NFL Championships: 1
Colors: Black, Purple, and Metallic Gold
Mascot: Poe

★

BALTIMORE RAVENS

DEE-FENSE!

The Ravens' interesting history began in 1996 when the Cleveland Browns moved to Baltimore. Though the team featured many of the same players and **front-office** personnel as the 1995 Cleveland team did, the Baltimore Ravens were considered a new team. The Browns' history, records, and uniforms all remained in Cleveland.

It didn't take long for the new team to get up to speed. By 2000, the Ravens had built a record-setting defense that carried them all the way to a Super Bowl victory. Since then, Baltimore has featured some of the NFL's best defenses.

In recent years, some new talent on offense has made the Ravens strong on the other side of the ball, too. A strong offense plus a strong defense equals a Super Bowl contender!

The Ravens drafted running back Ray Rice in 2008.

HOME FIELD

Baltimore fans get to watch their favorite sports teams play in two of the coolest pro stadiums. The same architects who designed Oriole Park at Camden Yards for the city's Major League Baseball team also designed M&T Bank Stadium for the Ravens.

BIG DAYS

- ★ In 2000, the Ravens allowed only 165 total points—the fewest by any NFL team in a 16-game season. Their defense was not going to be denied in Super Bowl XXXV against the New York Giants. Baltimore won 34–7.
- ★ Safety Ed Reed returned an interception an incredible 106 yards for a touchdown in a win over the Cleveland Browns in 2004. That was an NFL record until 2008, when Reed went 107 yards for a touchdown in a victory over the Philadelphia Eagles.

More than 70,000 fans can pack M&T Bank Stadium to cheer on the Ravens.

SUPERSTARS!

★

THEN

Peter Boulware, linebacker: hard-hitting defender who made the Pro Bowl four times

Jamal Lewis, running back: one of the few players ever to run for 2,000 yards in a season

Jonathan Ogden, tackle: anchored the offensive line for the club's first 12 years

★

NOW

Joe Flacco, quarterback: a starter and a winner since his rookie year in 2008

Ed Reed, safety: a big-play defensive back

Ray Rice, running back: a do-everything back

★

STAT LEADERS

(All-time team leaders*)

Passing Yards: Joe Flacco, 10,206

Rushing Yards: Jamal Lewis, 7,801

Receiving Yards: Derrick Mason, 5,777

Touchdowns: Jamal Lewis, 47

Interceptions: Ed Reed, 54

★

(*Through 2010 season)

TIMELINE

1996

Ravens begin playing in the AFC's Central Division.

2000

Ravens make the playoffs for the first time and beat the New York Giants to win Super Bowl XXXV.

2002

The team moves to the newly formed AFC North Division.

Quarterback Joe Flacco led the Ravens to a 17–10 victory against the Bengals in his first NFL game.

2003
Ravens are AFC North champions for the first time.

2006
The team wins a club-record thirteen games during the regular season.

2008
Baltimore advances to the AFC Championship Game but loses to Pittsburgh.

First Season: 1968
NFL Championships: 0
Colors: Black, Orange, and White
Mascot: Who Dey

★

CINCINNATI

BENGALS

A FRESH START

Legendary NFL coach Paul Brown had a team named after him: the Cleveland Browns. After leaving the Browns, Coach Brown wasn't ready to call it quits. In 1968, he started his own American Football League (AFL) **expansion team:** the Bengals. Two years later, the Bengals were in the NFL—and in the playoffs, too. The team won its last seven regular-season games in 1970 to earn a surprise **postseason** appearance in just its third season.

The Bengals had some powerful offenses in the 1980s. They won the AFC championship in 1981 and 1988. Both times, they lost to the San Francisco 49ers in the Super Bowl. The Bengals won a pair of AFC North titles in the 2000s. The team is still looking for its first Super Bowl championship.

Wide receiver Chad Ochocinco holds the Bengals team record for most seasons with more than 1,000 receiving yards.

HOME FIELD

The Bengals' home stadium, Paul Brown Stadium, is named after the team's founder. When the team scores, Cincinnati fans like to sing, "Who dey? Who dey? Who dey think gonna beat them Bengals?" It's not proper grammar, but it's a lot of fun!

BIG DAYS

- No one involved will ever forget the Bengals' 27–7 win over San Diego in the 1981 AFC title game. Not only did it send Cincinnati to its first Super Bowl, it was also one of the coldest NFL games ever. The temperature was −9 degrees Fahrenheit (−23 degrees Celsius) at kickoff!
- The Bengals completed only two passes in a game against Denver in 2000. That's because they didn't need to throw the ball! Corey Dillon rushed for 278 yards to set an NFL single-game record (which has since been broken) in Cincinnati's 31–21 win.

Paul Brown Stadium holds 65,515 seats inside an area of 1,850,000 square feet.

SUPERSTARS!

★

THEN

Ken Anderson, quarterback: accurate and efficient QB who led the Bengals to their first Super Bowl

Pete Johnson, running back: burly runner who was tough to stop

Anthony Muñoz, tackle: one of the best offensive linemen in NFL history

★

NOW

Cedric Benson, running back: key to clinching the 2009 division title with his first 1,000-yard season

Dhani Jones, linebacker: **prolific** tackler

Chad Ochocinco, wide receiver: the top pass catcher in franchise history

Carson Palmer, quarterback: strong-armed **signal caller**

★

STAT LEADERS

(All-time team leaders*)

Passing Yards: Ken Anderson, 32,838

Rushing Yards: Corey Dillon, 8,061

Receiving Yards: Chad Ochocinco, 10,783

Touchdowns: Pete Johnson, 70

Interceptions: Ken Riley, 65

★

(*Through 2010 season.)

TIMELINE

1968
Bengals begin as an expansion team in the AFL's Western Division.

1970
Bengals join the NFL and, in just their third season, make the playoffs for the first time.

1981
Cincinnati wins its first AFC championship but loses to San Francisco in Super Bowl XVI.

1988
Bengals play in their second Super Bowl (XXIII) but lose to the 49ers again.

Running back Cedric Benson joined the Bengals in 2008 after playing three seasons with the Chicago Bears.

2002

The team moves to the newly formed AFC North Division.

2005

Cincinnati ends a fifteen-year playoff drought by winning the AFC North championship for the first time.

2009

After winning only four games in 2008, the Bengals rack up ten wins for another division championship.

First Season: 1946
NFL Championships: 4
Colors: Brown, Orange, and White
Mascot: Chomps

★

CLEVELAND

BROWNS

A WINNING HISTORY

No pro football team has ever been as **dominant** as the Cleveland Browns of the late 1940s and early 1950s. The Browns started off in the All-America Football Conference (AAFC) in 1946. After winning championships in all four years of the AAFC's existence, the Browns moved to the NFL in 1950. They won the title their first year in that league, too! The team lost in the championship game the next three years, but then won it all again in 1954 and 1955.

After another championship in 1964, the Browns fell on hard times. Their fans remained among the most loyal in football, though. So it was a shock when the team moved to Baltimore after the 1995 season. After three seasons without an NFL team, Cleveland got the Browns back with an all-new team in 1999. The new Browns haven't had a lot of success yet, but some good young players give them hope for better days ahead!

The Browns selected quarterback Colt McCoy in the third round of the 2010 NFL Draft.

HOME FIELD

Browns fans cheer on their team at Cleveland Browns Stadium, which opened in 1999. In a tradition that has carried over from old Municipal Stadium, the most **rabid** fans sit in a section of the end zone called the "Dawg Pound."

BIG DAYS

- ★ When the Browns played defending champ Philadelphia in their first game in the league in 1950, many people predicted an easy win for Philadelphia. It was an easy win—but for Cleveland, not Philadelphia! The Browns won the game 35–10 and went on to win the championship that year.
- ★ The first victory for the "new Browns" in 1999 came on an amazing play. On the final snap, Tim Couch launched a long pass that was deflected by two defenders. Then, as time ran out, it was caught by receiver Kevin Johnson for a touchdown! Cleveland beat New Orleans 21–16.

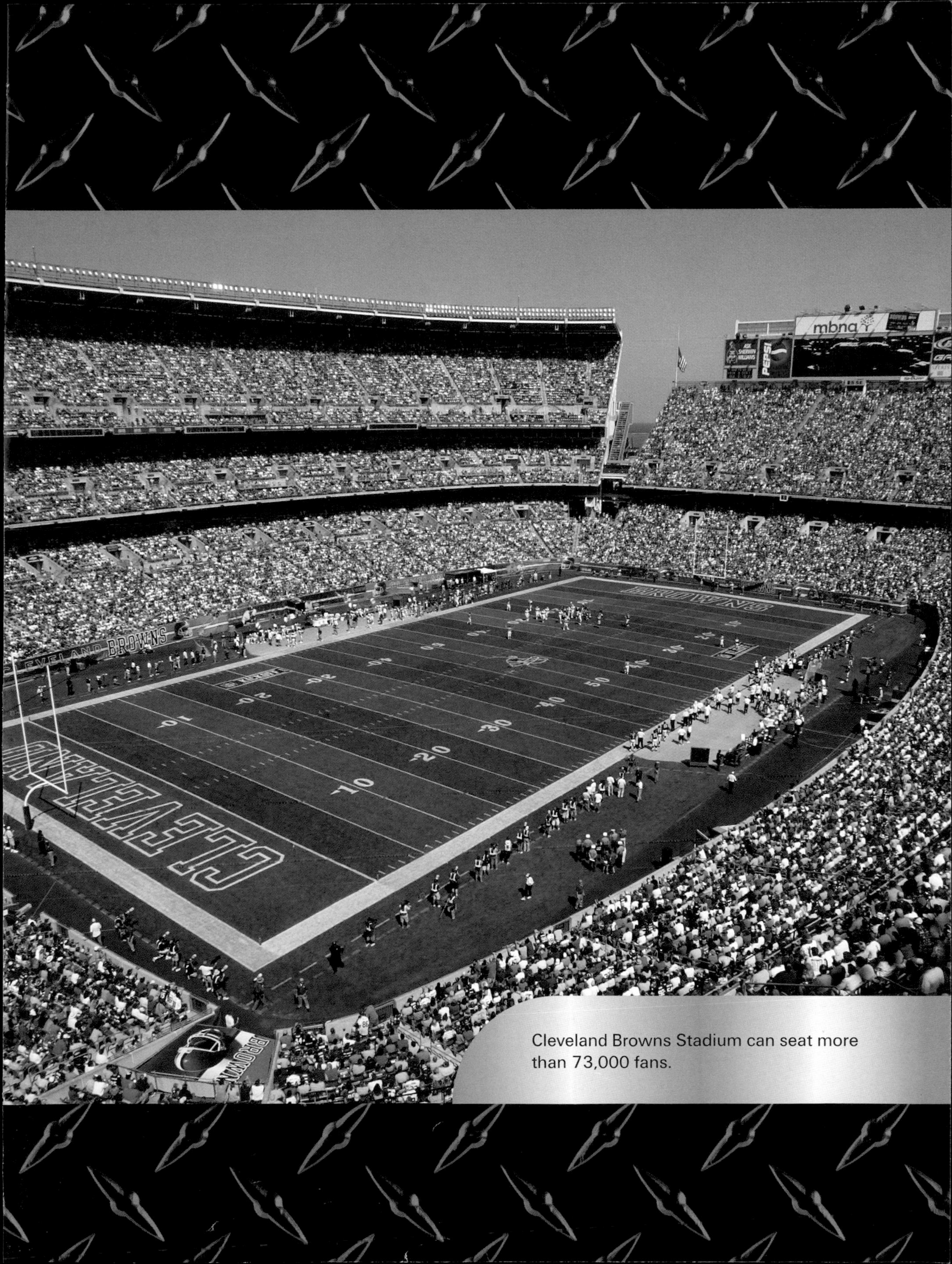

Cleveland Browns Stadium can seat more than 73,000 fans.

SUPERSTARS!

★

THEN

Jim Brown, running back: the league's top rusher eight times in nine NFL seasons

Otto Graham, quarterback: led the Browns to title games in each of his ten years

Lou Groza, tackle: big lineman who was also one of football's best kickers in his prime

★

NOW

Josh Cribbs, wide receiver: all-purpose player who can run, throw, catch, and return kicks

Colt McCoy, quarterback: 2010 rookie who made a huge impact

Joe Thomas, tackle: one of the best in the NFL

★

STAT LEADERS

(All-time team leaders*)

Passing Yards: Brian Sipe, 23,713

Rushing Yards: Jim Brown, 12,312

Receiving Yards: Ozzie Newsome, 7,980

Touchdowns: Jim Brown, 126

Interceptions: Thom Darden, 45

★

(*Through 2010 season.)

TIMELINE

1946
Browns begin play in the All-America Football Conference (AAFC) and win the first of four straight AAFC championships.

1950
Browns win the NFL title during their first year in the league.

1955
Browns win the NFL championship for the second year in a row and the third time in six years.

1964
Browns beat the Colts to win their fourth NFL title.

Wide receiver Josh Cribbs has an NFL record eight career kickoff return touchdowns.

1999

After Cleveland is without a team for nearly four years, the new Browns begin play in the AFC Central Division.

2002

Playing in the newly formed AFC North Division, Cleveland earns a wild-card playoff berth.

2007

The new Browns have their best season yet, winning ten games, but miss the playoffs on tiebreakers.

First Season: 1933
NFL Championships: 6
Colors: Black and Gold
Mascot: Steely McBeam

★

PITTSBURGH

STEELERS

THE PRIDE OF STEELTOWN

It took a long time for the Steelers to field a championship team. But ever since they did it for the first time, it's become quite a habit. In fact, the Steelers have now won the Super Bowl more times than any other team.

The Steelers began as the Pittsburgh Pirates in 1933, sharing a name with Pittsburgh's Major League Baseball team. In 1940, the team got its own identity when they were renamed the Steelers. The team hardly ever made the playoffs in its first 40 years and didn't capture a championship until winning Super Bowl IX in the 1974 season. A great defense nicknamed the "Steel Curtain" made the Steelers the best NFL team of the 1970s. Pittsburgh won the Super Bowl four times in six seasons.

The Steelers didn't stop there, though. They won two more championships in the 2000s to become the first NFL team with six Super Bowl wins.

Ben Roethlisberger was 23 years old during Super Bowl XL, making him the youngest starting quarterback in NFL history to win a Super Bowl.

HOME FIELD

The Steelers play at Heinz Field. It's named for a food company whose most famous product is ketchup, and it has giant ketchup bottles atop the scoreboard! Steelers fans wave bright gold towels called "Terrible Towels" to cheer on their team.

BIG DAYS

- ★ During the 1972 playoffs, the Steelers beat the Raiders 13–7 on perhaps the most famous play in NFL history. In the final seconds, Terry Bradshaw's long pass bounced off a defender and into the hands of running back Franco Harris, who finished off the winning 60-yard TD.
- ★ The Steelers won their most recent Super Bowl with another fantastic catch. In the final minute of Super Bowl XLIII against the Cardinals, Santonio Holmes leaped through three defenders, kept his feet in bounds, and held on to a six-yard touchdown for a 27–23 win.

Up to 65,050 fans can wave their Terrible Towels at Steelers home games.

SUPERSTARS!

★

THEN

Terry Bradshaw, quarterback: MVP of two Super Bowl wins in the 1970s

Joe Greene, defensive tackle: known as "Mean Joe" Greene

Franco Harris, running back: the franchise's all-time leading rusher

★

NOW

James Harrison, linebacker: made a huge interception return for a key TD in Super Bowl XLIII

Troy Polamalu, safety: Steelers' defense is always better—a lot better—when he plays

Ben Roethlisberger, quarterback: "Big Ben" has led the team to a pair of Super Bowl wins

★

STAT LEADERS

(All-time team leaders*)

Passing Yards: Terry Bradshaw, 27,989

Rushing Yards: Franco Harris, 11,950

Receiving Yards: Hines Ward, 11,702

Touchdowns: Franco Harris, 100

Interceptions: Mel Blount, 57

★

(*Through 2010 season.)

TIMELINE

1933
The team plays its first season as the Pittsburgh Pirates in the NFL's Eastern Division.

1947
Pittsburgh ties for the division championship but loses a playoff game to the Eagles.

1972
Pittsburgh wins its first division title and beats the Raiders in a playoff game on Franco Harris' famous catch.

1974
Steelers beat the Minnesota Vikings in Super Bowl IX to win their first league title.

Beginning in 2004, safety Troy Polamalu was selected to play in five consecutive Pro Bowls.

1979

Victory over the Rams in Super Bowl XIV gives Pittsburgh its fourth NFL title in six seasons.

2002

Steelers win the championship in the AFC North's first season.

2005

Pittsburgh beats Seattle to win Super Bowl XL.

2008

Steelers beat the Cardinals to become the first team to win six Super Bowls

STAT STUFF

★

AFC NORTH DIVISION STATISTICS*

Team	All-Time Record (W-L-T)	NFL Titles (Most Recent)	Times in NFL Playoffs
Baltimore Ravens	137–117–1	1 (2000)	7
Cincinnati Bengals	291–381–2	0	9
Cleveland Browns	449–414–10	4 (1964)	24
Pittsburgh Steelers	579–533–21	6 (2008)	26

★

AFC NORTH DIVISION CHAMPIONSHIPS (MOST RECENT)

Baltimore Ravens . . . 2 (2006)
Cincinnati Bengals . . . 2 (2009)
Cleveland Browns . . . 0
Pittsburgh Steelers . . . 5 (2010)

★

(*Through 2010 season.)

Position Key:
QB: Quarterback
RB: Running back
WR: Wide receiver
C: Center
T: Tackle
G: Guard
K: Kicker
CB: Cornerback
LB: Linebacker
DE: Defensive end
DB: Defensive back
DL: Defensive line
DT: Defensive tackle
TE: Tight end

AFC NORTH PRO FOOTBALL HALL OF FAME MEMBERS

Baltimore Ravens

Rod Woodson, DB

Cincinnati Bengals

Charlie Joiner, WR
Anthony Muñoz, T

Cleveland Browns

Jim Brown, RB
Paul Brown, Coach
Joe DeLamielleure, G
Len Ford, DE
Frank Gatski, C
Otto Graham, QB
Lou Groza, T, K
Gene Hickerson, G
Leroy Kelly, RB
Dante Lavelli, WR
Mike McCormack, T
Bobby Mitchell, RB, WR
Marion Motley, RB
Ozzie Newsome, TE
Paul Warfield, WR
Bill Willis, DL

Pittsburgh Steelers

Bert Bell, Owner
Mel Blount, CB
Terry Bradshaw, QB
Len Dawson, QB
Bill Dudley, RB
Joe Greene, DT
Jack Ham, LB
Franco Harris, RB
John Henry Johnson, RB
Walt Kiesling, G, Coach
Jack Lambert, LB
Bobby Layne, QB
John (Blood) McNally, RB
Chuck Noll, Coach
Art Rooney, Owner
Dan Rooney, Owner
John Stallworth, WR
Ernie Stautner, DT
Lynn Swann, WR
Mike Webster, C
Rod Woodson, DB

NOTE: Includes players with at least three seasons with the team. Players may appear with more than one team.

GLOSSARY

dominant (DOM-uh-nuhnt): superior or powerful

expansion team (ek-SPAN-shuhn TEEM): new team added to an existing league

front office (FRUHNT OFF-iss): the administrators of a sports team

legendary (LEJ-uhn-dar-ee): famous for past accomplishments

postseason (pohst-SEE zuhn): playoffs, including the Super Bowl

prolific (pruh-LIF-ik): very productive

rabid (RAB-id): passionate

signal caller (SIG-nuhl CAWL-ur): quarterback

FIND OUT MORE

★

BOOKS

Buckley, James Jr. *Scholastic Ultimate Guide to Football.* New York: Scholastic, 2009.

Jacobs, Greg. *The Everything Kids' Football Book.* Avon, MA: Adams Media, 2010.

MacRae, Sloan. *The Pittsburgh Steelers.* New York: PowerKids, 2010.

Stewart, Mark. *The Baltimore Ravens.* Chicago,: Norwood House Press, 2009.

Stewart, Mark. *The Cincinnati Bengals.* Chicago: Norwood House Press, 2009.

Stewart, Mark. *The Cleveland Browns.* Chicago: Norwood House, Press, 2007.

Whiting, Jim. *Troy Polamalu.* Broomall, PA: Mason Crest Publishers, 2009.

★

WEB SITES

For links to learn more about football visit

www.childsworld.com/links

Note to Parents, Teachers, and Librarians: We routinely verify our Web links to make sure they are safe and active sites. So encourage your readers to check them out!

INDEX

★

ABOUT THE AUTHOR

Jim Gigliotti is a freelance writer based in Southern California. A former editor at the National Football League, he has written more than fifty books on sports for children and adults.